T0372613

Cambridge Early Years

Communication and Language

for English as a First Language

Learner's Book 2A

Gill Budgell

Contents

Note to parents and practitioners

This Learner's Book provides activities to support the first term of FLE Communication and Language for Cambridge Early Years 2.

Activities can be used at school or at home. Children will need support from an adult. Additional guidance about activities can be found in the **For practitioners** boxes.

Stories are provided for children to enjoy looking at and listening to. Children are not expected to be able to read the stories themselves.

Children will encounter the following characters within this book. You could ask children to point to the characters when they see them on the pages, and say their names.

The Learner's Book activities support the Teaching Resource activities. The Teaching Resource provides step-by-step coverage of the Cambridge Early Years curriculum and guidance on how the Learner's Book activities develop the curriculum learning statements.

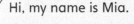
Hi, my name is Mia.

Find us on the front covers doing lots of fun activities.

Hi, my name is Gemi.

Hi, my name is Rafi.

Hi, my name is Kiho.

Special to Me

Look at me and my family! *(arms to self then out)*

Can you count along with me? *(wriggle fingers)*

Mum is one and Dad makes two,

Here is my brother looking at you!

Then I have a baby small,

She looks sweet but WOW, can she BAWL!

Look at me and my family!

Everyone is special to me.

Look at me and my family!

Can you count along with me?

Aunty is one and Uncle makes two,

Here is my cousin smiling at you!

Then I have a Grandpa old,

To us all he is pure gold!

Look at me and my family!

Everyone is special to me.

Look at me and my family!

Did you count along with me?

Mum … 1

Dad … 2

Brother … 3

Baby small … 4

Aunty … 5

Uncle … 6

Cousin … 7

Grandpa old … 8

Me … NUMBER 9!

Look at me and my family!

Everyone is special to me.

Pure gold

Create.

Stick gold scraps to make a gold picture.

My gold picture by _____

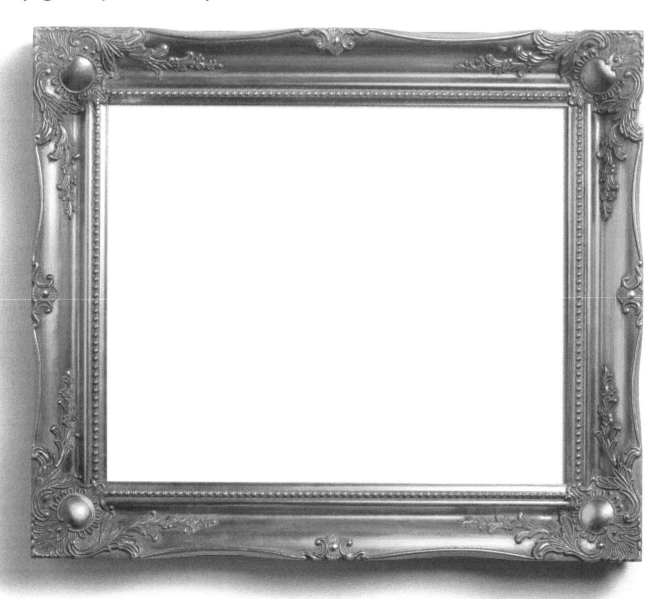

For practitioners

Provide children with a selection of scraps (paper, fabric, leaves) in golden colours. They select scraps to stick in their book to make their own gold picture. Encourage talk about the colour in relation to the text and about the scraps they have chosen.

Special to me

Draw and say.

Who at home is special to you?
Draw and talk about them.

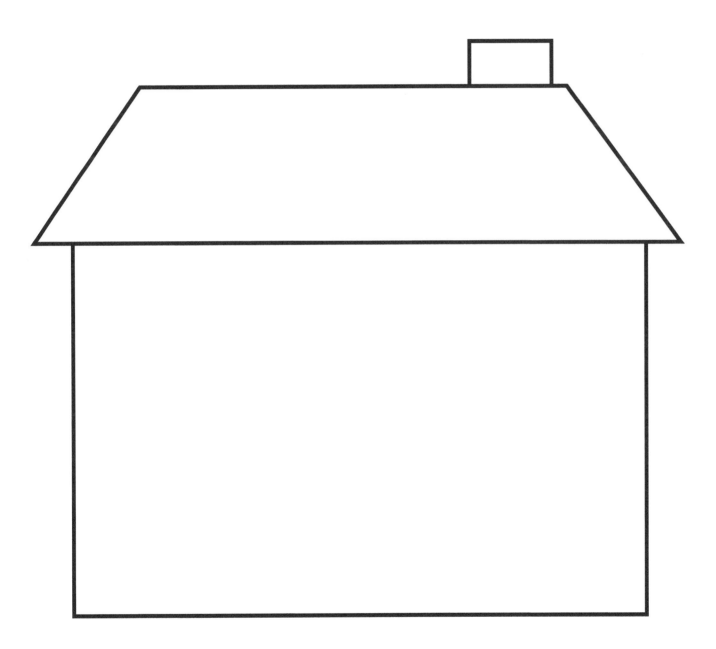

For practitioners
Encourage children to talk about why this person is special to them.
If they are able, ask them to write down the person's name.

Around the Table That Grandad Built

by Melanie Heuiser Hill

This is the table that Grandad built.
These are the sunflowers picked by my cousins
Set on the table that Grandad built.

These are the napkins sewn by Mom
Surrounding the sunflowers picked by my cousins
Set on the table that Grandad built.

These are our plates – red, orange, and yellow …
That go with the napkins sewn by Mom
Surrounding the sunflowers picked by my cousins
Set on the table that Grandad built.

These are the glasses from Mom and Dad's wedding ...
Set by our plates – red, orange, and yellow –
That go with the napkins sewn by Mom
Surrounding the sunflowers picked by my cousins
Set on the table that Grandad built.

These are the forks and spoons and knives –
gifts from Dad's grandma long ago ...
Placed by the glasses from Mom and Dad's wedding
Set by our plates – red, orange, and yellow –
That go with the napkins sewn by Mom
Surrounding the sunflowers picked by my cousins
Set on the table that Grandad built.

This is the squash that took over our garden.
These are the potatoes and peppers we roasted.
And these are the beans, overflowing the bowl!

This is the stack of toasty tamales.
These are the samosas, spicy and hot.
And this is the rice pudding we have every year.

This is the bread – still warm! – that Gran baked.
This is the butter made by us kids.
And this is Dad's huckleberry jam –
mmmMMMMMM.
And *here* are the pies! I made this one myself!

For these hands we hold, for tasty
good food, for family and friends,
For grace that is given and love that
is shared, we give thanks …
Around this table that Grandad built.

What's on the table?

Circle and say.

Talk about the picture.
Circle and say the things on the table.

Shadow pictures

Match and say.

Join each shadow to its colour picture with a line. Say its name.

spoon

sunflowers

tamale

rice pudding

samosa

fork

beans

glass

squash

For practitioners

Children draw a line to match the shadows to the correct items in colour. Ask them to name the items as they do this. It may help to run your finger under each label as you help them to read.

What's on your table?

Draw and write.

Write your name in the gap.

The table that _____ built

Draw what you would have on your party table.

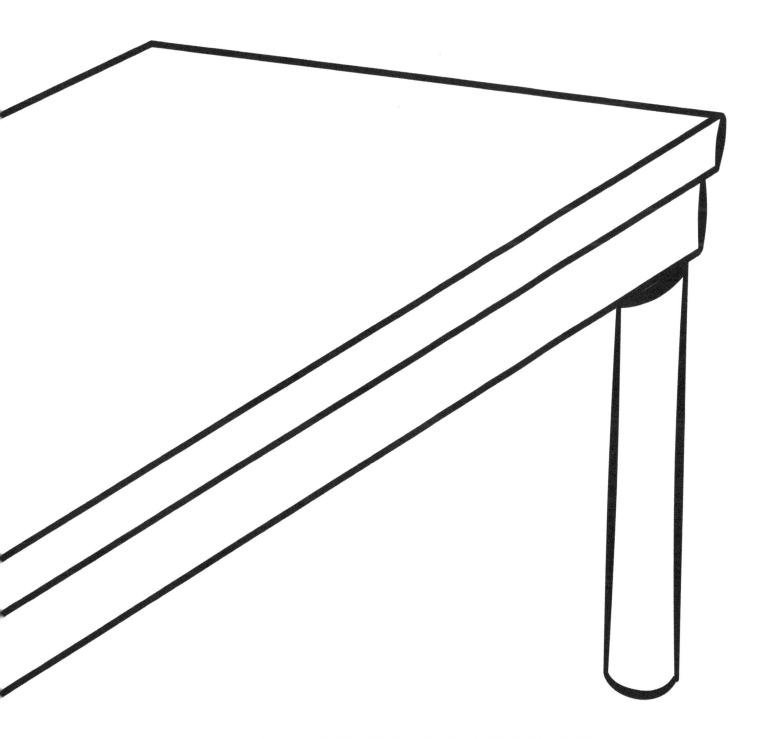

For practitioners

Children attempt to write their name in the sentence gap. They talk about and draw the items they would like to include on their party table.

Set on the table that Grandad built

Trace and say.

Trace the letters. Say the words.

Set on the *table* that Grandad built.

Picture talk

Point and say.

Listen to the questions and
say the answers.

1   How many people are lifting the table?
2   Find and point to this in the picture. ⟶
    Who do you think is in the photo?
3   What can you see next to the photo?
    How do you know?

For practitioners

Read the questions aloud to the children. Children point to the picture and say their responses.
Encourage them to talk about their responses. Possible answers to the questions include:
1) Five people. 2) Grandad and Grandma. 3) A plant. We can see some leaves.

This is the Way

(to the tune of *Here We Go Round the Mulberry Bush*)

This is the way we play football,
play football, play football.
This is the way we play football,
on a bright and sunny morning!

This is the way we roller skate,
roller skate, roller skate.
This is the way we roller skate,
on a bright and sunny morning!

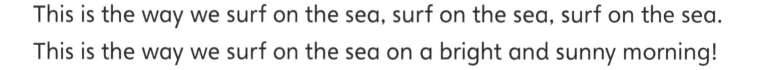

This is the way we surf on the sea, surf on the sea, surf on the sea.
This is the way we surf on the sea on a bright and sunny morning!

This is the way we strike a ball, strike a ball, strike a ball.
This is the way we strike a ball on a bright and sunny morning!

This is the way we run a race, run a race, run a race.
This is the way we run a race on a bright and sunny morning!

This is the way I ...

Choose and say.

Use the pictures to make up your own song.
Add actions.

Learning to Surf by Jason Cole

Last summer, I stayed at my Gran's. She has a house by the sea. That was the summer that I learnt to surf.

My Dad gave me his old surfboard so I jumped right in. The waves were quite big so I jumped right out again.

My sister gave me some advice. "Balance" she said, "Surfing is all about balance." So with this in mind, I tried again.

Her advice was not as useful as I thought. The only time that I was balanced was when I was on the beach.

My brother said that it's all in your diet. But I found that hard to believe, judging from what he puts into his stomach.

I should have had a lighter lunch, because I spent the next day at the bottom of the sea.

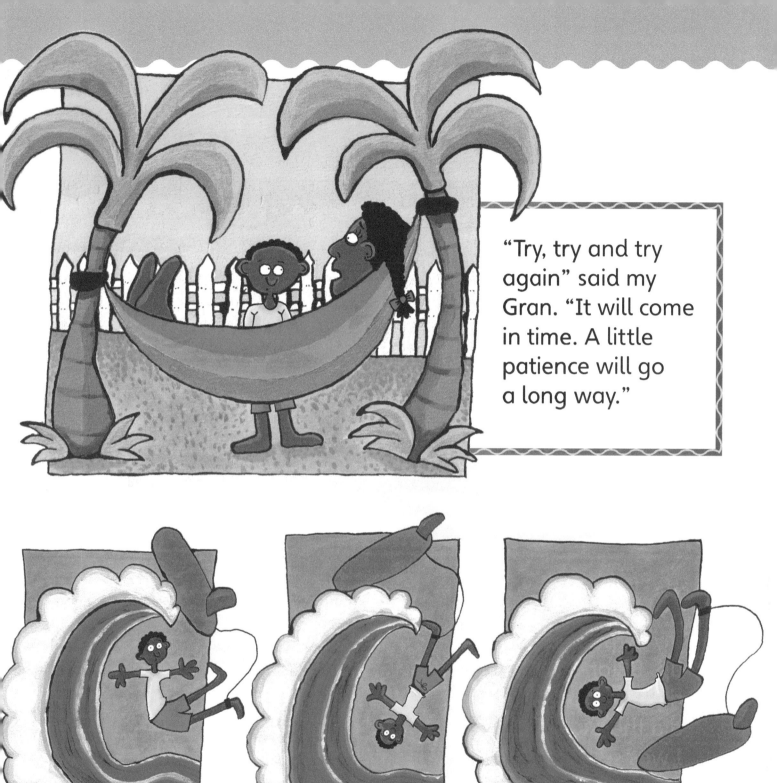

"Try, try and try again" said my Gran. "It will come in time. A little patience will go a long way."

Try … try … and try again.

I decided to take it slowly and spend the next day snorkelling. You can learn a lot about the ocean when you're under it.

The next day I stood up and to my surprise, I stayed up. Balance, eating right and patience did the trick. I was surfing.

Now I surf almost every day and I love it. Some day I will win a surfing trophy. All of my hard work has paid off.

Maybe next summer I will teach my little sister how to surf. She thinks that she already can.

Listen and respond

Listen to the story.

Draw a line to join the pictures in the right order.

For practitioners

Look at the pictures and explain they are in the wrong order. Read the story again and ask children to listen carefully. As they listen, they draw lines to join the pictures in the correct order. Encourage children to use the joined pictures to retell the story.

Can you do this?

Think.

Look at each picture. Do you think you could balance like this? Tick ✓ for yes or cross ✗ for no.

Spot the crab

Match and say.

Look and the crab and say what it is doing.
Point to the matching picture from the story.

staying at Gran's house by the sea

surfing

under the sea

balancing

winning

What did Gran say?

Trace and write.

Read the words with help.
Trace them and write them.

Try, try and

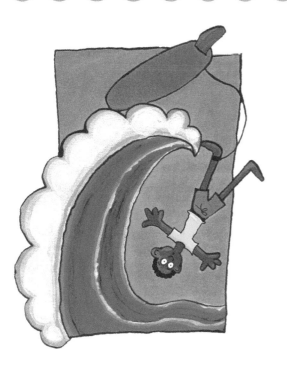

try again.

For practitioners
Encourage children to read, trace and then copy Gran's advice. Check their pencil grips and direction.
Children can read back the sentence. Provide support if needed. Ask *What does it mean to 'Try, try and try again'?*

31

Acknowledgements

The authors and publishers acknowledge the following sources of copyright material and are grateful for the permissions granted.
While every effort has been made, it has not always been possible to identify the sources of all the material used, or to trace all copyright holders.
If any omissions are brought to our notice, we will be happy to include the appropriate acknowledgements on reprinting.

AROUND THE TABLE THAT GRANDAD BUILT Text © 2019 Melanie Heuiser Hill, Illustrations © 2019 Jimyung Kim.
Written by Melanie Heuiser Hill & Illustrated by Jimyung Kim. Reproduced by permission
of Walker Books Ltd, London, SE11 5HJ www.walker.co.uk

Learning to Surf © Jason Cole 2023

Thanks to the following for permission to reproduce images:
p6 Peter Dazeley/Getty Images

Thanks to the following artists at Beehive Illustration:
Laura Arias, John Lund, Tamara Joubert.

Cover characters by Becky Davies (The Bright Agency)